Ladders

The U.S. Constitution
Famous Documents

MEET THE
CON

by Sheri Reda

What if no one were in charge at your school or in your classroom? School would be a crazy place with no control. It's the same for our country. We have a government, laws, and rules to keep order. A country couldn't survive without a government making sure that life is fair and society works well. Without a government, there would be no order.

This country's Founders knew the importance of a strong government. More than 200 years ago, they wrote the U.S. Constitution. This document set up our federal government. In the part of the Constitution called the Articles, the United States is set up as a **republic** in which people elect representatives. The Constitution also created three equal branches to balance power. These branches work together to make and carry out the laws. The photo and captions on the right identify these branches—the executive, legislative, and judicial branches.

THE EXECUTIVE BRANCH

In January 2013, Barack Obama was sworn in for his second term as president in Washington, D.C. President Obama took the **oath** of office. He promised to preserve, protect, and defend the Constitution. As head of the executive branch, the president can sign bills into law and **veto**, or reject, bills. The president is also the commander-in-chief of the Armed Forces.

President Obama

∧ President Barack Obama is joined by his wife, First Lady Michelle Obama, and their two daughters as he takes the oath of office for the second time.

STITUTION

THE LEGISLATIVE BRANCH

Representative John Boehner and Senator Chuck Schumer looked on as President Obama took the oath of office. Both work in the U.S. Congress, the legislative branch. Congress is made up of the Senate and the House of Representatives. The elected officials in Congress introduce, review, and pass bills before the bills come to the president to be signed into law or vetoed.

Representative Boehner

Senator Schumer

THE JUDICIAL BRANCH

Chief Justice John Roberts administered the oath to the president. Roberts leads the other eight judges who make up the Supreme Court, which is part of the judicial branch. The Supreme Court decides whether laws are fair and makes sure they follow the Constitution.

Chief Justice Roberts

3

A CLOSER LOOK

Our Constitution brings us together as a country and guarantees that all U.S. citizens enjoy the same rights. It has guided our government since 1787. But it has been changed many times to reflect changes in how we live. Let's take a closer look at our Constitution and its updates.

THE PREAMBLE

"We the People" are the first words of the Constitution's preamble, or introduction. Who are "the People"? The definition has changed over time. Today, all adult citizens make up "the People." They elect the country's leaders. That's what makes our government a republic.

THE ARTICLES

The Constitution's seven articles, or sections, describe how our government works. The first three of these articles set up the government's legislative, executive, and judicial branches.

THE AMENDMENTS

Over time, changes called **amendments** have been added to the Constitution. Here are the 27 amendments. The first ten amendments are called the Bill of Rights. The Bill of Rights spells out basic individual rights. The original wording of the amendments is hard to read, so we'll look at them in easier language.

1. You have the right to freedom of religion, assembly, petition, the press, and speech. (1791)

2. You have the right to bear arms. (1791)

3. You cannot be forced to allow soldiers to stay in your home during peacetime. (1791)

4. You have the right to be safe from unreasonable searches and seizures, which means that police or other government officials cannot search you or your home for no reason. (1791)

5. You have the right to due process of law. That includes the right to remain silent and not testify against yourself if you are arrested. (1791)

6. If accused of a crime, you have the right to a lawyer and a speedy and fair trial. (1791)

7. You have the right to trial by jury. (1791)

8. You have the right to be safe from cruel punishment and excessive fines. (1791)

9. You have other rights besides those listed in the Constitution. (1791)

10. Powers that the Constitution does not give to the U.S. government go instead to state governments. (1791)

11. The United States has no power in lawsuits against individual states. (1795)

12. Representatives called electors meet in their states and cast two votes—one for president and one for vice-president. (1804)

13. Slavery is banned. (1865)

14. No state can take away the rights of U.S. citizens. (1868)

15. U.S. citizens cannot be denied the right to vote because of race. (1870)

16. The U.S. government can collect taxes on money people earn. (1913)

17. The people of each state elect two U.S. senators, who serve for six years. (1913)

18. It is illegal to make, sell, or transport alcoholic beverages. (1919)

19. Women have the right to vote. (1920)

20. Each elected president takes office on January 20th of the year following the election. (1933)

21. The 18th Amendment is struck down, making it legal to make, sell, and transport alcoholic drinks. (1933)

22. A president can serve only two terms in office. (1951)

23. The people of Washington, D.C., can vote in elections for president. (1961)

24. Citizens have the right to vote without paying any taxes or fees for that right. (1964)

25. If the president dies or is unable to perform the duties of office, the vice-president takes over. (1967)

26. Citizens have the right to vote at age 18 or older. (1971)

27. If members of Congress vote to raise their own pay, the raise begins after the next election. (1992)

Check In Why is the Constitution so important to our country?

Read to find out about the debates that helped shape the U.S. Constitution.

Conflict and Compromise

by Becky Manfredini   illustrated by John Jay Cabuay

> Welcome, everyone! James Madison at your service. They call me the "Father of the Constitution." I'll be your guide as you see how Founders like me created that document.

In 1787, leaders of every state except Rhode Island met in Philadelphia, Pennsylvania. They met to make a new plan, or constitution, for the United States. For six years, the government had been guided by the Articles of Confederation. Under that plan, the government could not form an army or collect taxes. Representatives at this Constitutional **Convention** needed to create a stronger government. But they did not agree on how to form our legislature, or lawmaking body. Small states wanted a legislature with the same number of representatives from each state. That way, each state would have equal power. Large states with more people wanted to have more representatives and more power.

The only way to give the people a voice is to base the number of representatives from a state on how many people live in that state!

That is unfair and unacceptable. Every state should have an equal number of representatives, no matter how big or small it is!

New Jersey Delegates

Virginia Delegates

The small states and large states reached a **compromise**. Each side agreed to give up something to reach an agreement. According to the compromise, we agreed to have two lawmaking bodies. One would be the House of Representatives, based on the number of people in each state. The other would be the Senate, with two representatives from each state. And so, with this compromise, we had some peace for a while.

The next argument was about how many representatives each state would have in the House of Representatives. We had agreed that the number would be based on the population of the states. But should enslaved people be counted? Southern states wanted to count enslaved people. That way, those states would get more representatives—and more power.

You don't count enslaved people as citizens, so you can't count them as part of your population!

Northern Delegates

We overcame many challenges as we created the Constitution. The biggest one came at the end of our convention. We needed two-thirds of the states to **ratify**, or approve, the Constitution. Some delegates supported the Constitution as we had written it. Others thought it gave too much control to the U.S. government, and they wanted a list of basic rights for individuals. They had an idea about how to address these problems and change the Constitution.

I'm afraid this constitution gives too much power to the U.S. government. We need a list of rights to protect the people.

No we don't. The three branches of government have separate powers, and these branches will protect the rights of the people. Anyway, there are too many individual rights to list them all separately.

We added a Bill of Rights to the Constitution. The ten amendments in the Bill of Rights protect citizens' basic human rights, such as freedom of religion, speech, and press. On March 4, 1789, the first Congress and President George Washington took office under the new Constitution. I knew this document would guide our nation for many years.

Check In What was one compromise the leaders of the states made as they wrote the U.S. Constitution?

WE THE PEOPLE

by Becky Manfredini

In this painting, *Scene at the Signing of the Constitution of the United States* (1940), state representatives sign the new U.S. Constitution.

Our Constitution is a great document, but it is not perfect. The Founders realized that as times change, our Constitution might need to change too. They made sure that the citizens of the United States could amend the U.S. Constitution, but they didn't make it easy. Amendments must be passed by Congress and ratified, or approved, by two-thirds of the states. Only 17 amendments have been added since the Bill of Rights, for a total of 27. These 17 amendments reflect important issues in U.S. history. Let's see why some of the amendments were made.

13th, 14th

FREE AT LAST!

The Thirteenth, Fourteenth, and Fifteenth Amendments were passed in the 1800s. They were added to meet the needs of some of those not originally included in "We the People." Those are the first three words of the Preamble to the Constitution. The Founders could not solve the problem of slavery in the United States when they wrote the Constitution. All people were not equal citizens, were not allowed to vote, and did not have basic rights. It took a long, bloody war to end slavery.

The war was the Civil War, which began in 1861. This war between the states started in part because of slavery. People in the Southern states claimed they needed enslaved people to work their farms. People in the Northern states did not allow slavery. Conflict over the issue led the South to break away from the United States. It formed its own country and went to war with the Northern states.

The North won the war in 1865, and the country was reunited. Within five years, three new amendments became law. First, President Abraham Lincoln signed the Thirteenth Amendment in 1865. It abolished, or ended, slavery. Then the Fourteenth Amendment granted citizenship to formerly enslaved people in 1868. In 1870, the Fifteenth Amendment gave African American men the right to vote. But it would take almost another 100 years to grant all African Americans true **civil rights**, including the right to equal education, employment, and housing.

These newly freed African Americans were among about four million people freed by the Thirteenth Amendment.

5th Amendment

13

THE RISE AND FALL OF AN AMENDMENT

The Eighteenth Amendment passed in 1919. Then it was struck down by the Twenty-First Amendment in 1933. Here's what happened. In 1919, religious groups and women's groups blamed alcoholic drinks, such as beer and whiskey, for destroying families. They demanded prohibiting, or not allowing, the sale of alcoholic drinks. In response, the government passed the Eighteenth Amendment. It made making, selling, and transporting alcoholic drinks illegal. This ban was called **Prohibition**.

But Prohibition caused new problems. Many restaurants went out of business because they weren't able to sell alcohol.

This is a typical Prohibition scene. Here, police are emptying barrels of beer and other alcoholic beverages into the public sewer.

18th Amendment

Also, because of Prohibition, people lost jobs as servers, truckers, and factory workers. States that were used to collecting taxes from liquor sales suddenly couldn't pay their bills.

The growth of organized crime was the worst result of Prohibition. Criminals formed gangs to supply people with illegal alcoholic drinks. Gangsters such as Al Capone made money by selling illegal alcohol in the 1920s and 1930s. Violence rose as gangs fought each other. Instead of making people safer, the ban on alcohol made things worse. So the government gave up on Prohibition. In 1933, Congress passed the Twenty-First Amendment to **repeal**, or end, Prohibition. The Eighteenth Amendment is the only amendment ever to be repealed.

∨ This woman is expressing her support for an end to Prohibition.

VOTES FOR ALL CITIZENS!

The Nineteenth, Twenty-Fourth, and Twenty-Sixth Amendments brought voting rights to new groups.

Like African Americans, women had to wait until an amendment gave them **suffrage**, or the right to vote. For years, many women were arrested for speaking out for their rights. Finally in 1920, the Nineteenth Amendment gave women in the United States the right to vote. The nation had 26 million new voters.

Before 1964, African Americans in many states had to take a test before they could vote or pay a "poll tax," which is a charge for voting. This made voting

∨ People who supported women's voting rights were called suffragists. These suffragists are marching in New York City in 1917.

difficult. In January 1964, Congress passed the Twenty-Fourth Amendment. It made these unfair practices illegal.

One more group was dissatisfied with their voting rights: 18-year-old Americans. In the 1960s and 1970s, the United States fought a war in Vietnam. Vietnam is a country in Southeast Asia. Any 18-year-old American man could be drafted to fight in the war. Thousands fought and died in Vietnam. Yet, according to the U.S. Constitution, no one under the age of 21 could vote.

Many people pointed out that if 18-year-olds were old enough to fight in a war, they should also be allowed to vote. The Twenty-Sixth Amendment passed in 1971. It lowered the voting age for all Americans to 18.

A county clerk instructs an 18-year-old in how to use a voting machine so she can exercise her right to vote.

24th, 26th Amendments

Check In Which amendment in the selection did you find most interesting? Why was it important?

Failure Is Impossible

by Rosemary H. Knower

My wife's joined the Suffrage Movement,
(I've suffered ever since!)

Many cartoons of the 1800s and early 1900s made fun of suffragists, or people who fought for women's right to vote.

On August 26, 1995, the play "Failure Is Impossible" was read in Washington, D.C. It was read to celebrate the 75th anniversary of the Nineteenth Amendment. It tells the story of women's fight for voting rights.

Cast of Characters:

Narrator   Reader 1   Reader 2   Reader 3

SUFFRAGETTE SERIES N° 12.

OFFICIAL BALLOT

I LOVE MY HUSBAND, BUT—
OH YOU VOTE
COPYRIGHTED

Narrator: Today is the 75th anniversary of the passage of the Nineteenth Amendment, which gave women the right to vote. Did I hear you say, wait a minute—the country is 219 years old, and women have only been voting for 75 years? What's the problem here? It began with the words of the Founding Fathers: not the ones they put in, but the one they left out—"women." In 1776, when John Adams sat with a committee of men in Philadelphia, writing the Declaration of Independence, his wife Abigail wrote him:

Reader 1: John, in the new code of laws . . . remember the ladies. . . . Do not put such unlimited power in the hands of the husbands. Remember all men would be tyrants if they could. . . . We . . . will not hold ourselves bound by any laws in which we have no voice, or representation.

Narrator: But when the Founding Fathers wrote the Declaration and the Constitution, they stated: "We hold these truths to be self-evident, that all *men* are created equal." As a result, as of 1776, women could not vote or own property, and they had very few rights.

Songs and sayings helped motivate women during their fight for the right to vote. This is the cover for sheet music that was published in 1916.

Narrator: In 1848, a group of women organized the first Women's Rights Convention in Seneca Falls, New York. It took great courage. In the 1840s, respectable women did not even speak in public, let alone call meetings. Convention leader Elizabeth Cady Stanton said later:

Reader 1: We felt as helpless and hopeless as if we had suddenly been asked to construct a steam engine.

Narrator: But they were determined. They rewrote the Declaration of Independence to read: "We hold these truths to be self-evident: that all *men and women* are created equal." If women had the right to vote, they could defend themselves against men who took their wages or hurt them or their children. They needed more rights.

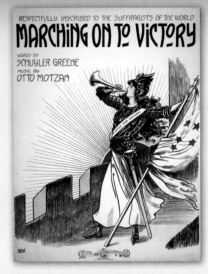

"Marching to Victory," was a song dedicated to suffragists around the world.

By 1900, over three million women worked for wages outside the home, often in hazardous and **exploitive** conditions, often with their children beside them at the machinery. They needed the ballot to give them a voice in making labor laws.

In the Triangle Shirtwaist Factory fire in 1911, 129 women were killed trying to escape an unsafe building into which they had been locked to keep them at work. Working women rushed to join the suffragist cause. With this new army of supporters, women succeeded in getting states to have **referendums**, or votes on one single issue—the issue of women's suffrage.

Reader 1: In 1912, the suffrage referendum was passed in Arizona, Kansas, and Oregon.

Reader 2: But defeated in Michigan, Ohio, and Wisconsin.

Narrator: In 1913, 5,000 women marched down Pennsylvania Avenue, in Washington, D.C., on the day before President Woodrow Wilson's inauguration, asking for the right to vote. They were mobbed by an angry crowd.

Reader 1: In 1914, the suffrage referendum passed in Montana and Nevada.

Reader 2: Defeated in North and South Dakota, Nebraska, and Missouri.

Reader 3: 1915: The suffrage referendum failed in New York, New Jersey, Pennsylvania, and Massachusetts.

Narrator: When the United States entered World War I in 1917, the government urged women to put aside their cause to help the war effort, just as the government had at the beginning of the Civil War in 1860. But in 1917, women worked for the war, and they also continued to work for the vote.

Reader 3 (reading from an eyewitness article)**:** In New York, more than a million women signed a **petition** asking for the right to vote. The petitions were pasted on signs carried by women marchers. The procession of the petitions alone covered more than half a mile.

Narrator: That same year, in Washington, D.C., other suffragists picketed outside the White House in rain and cold.

Reader 2: (Suffragist): Day after day, an intense silence would fall as the picketers were arrested. The watchers . . . saw not only younger women, but white-haired grandmothers, hoisted into the crowded patrol [wagon], their heads erect, and their frail hands holding tightly to the banner until [it was] wrested from them by brute force.

This was the cover of the official program of the women's suffrage march in 1913. Some onlookers made fun of the marchers.

This stamp and booklet urged Americans to give women the right to vote. The movement asked Americans to support women's suffrage with their votes.

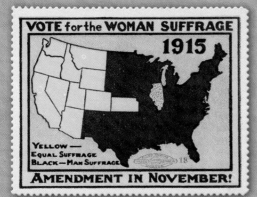

We are ready
to Work beside You, Fight
beside You and Die beside You

Let Us Vote beside You

VOTE FOR

Candidates for the legislature
who stand for

WOMAN
SUFFRAGE

Women
Working
in
Munition
Factory

Posters like this one asked voters to support candidates who would work for women's suffrage.

American Women

are urged to work in

Munition Plants
Railway Yards
Land Armies
Elevators
Trolley Cars
Ambulance Driving
Red Cross
Nursing, Etc.

BUT in most
States They
are NOT
trusted
To Vote

Enemy Aliens

are NOT trusted to work in

Munition Plants

Nor in many other war activities

BUT They ARE TRUSTED To Vote

In Eight States Foreigners Vote on First Papers.
In Nebraska in one County alone 785 men Claimed
Exemption from the Draft because they were
"Enemy Aliens," But Admitted They Had Voted
for years.

FOR THE HOME DEFENSE

Support those Candidates for the Legislature Who Stand for Woman Suffrage

During World War I, women worked in many jobs important to the nation's defense.
But they could not vote.

Narrator: The White House pickets kept public attention focused on the issue. In 1917, at the height of World War I, President Wilson spoke to urge the Congress to act on suffrage.

Reader 3 (President Woodrow Wilson)**:** This is a people's war. Women think that democracy means that they should play their part alongside men and upon an equal footing with them.

Narrator: In January of 1918, the Nineteenth Amendment to give women the right to vote came before the House. However, it would be another year before the Senate passed the suffrage amendment, and another year beyond that before the necessary 36 states would ratify it.

Finally, on August 26, 1920, the Nineteenth Amendment gave women across the United States the right to vote. At the last Suffrage Convention of 1920, suffragist Carrie Chapman Catt spoke to the joyful women:

Reader 2: Ours has been a movement with a soul. Women came, served, and passed on, but others came to take their places. Who shall say that all the hosts of the millions of women who have toiled and hoped and met delay are not here today, and joining in the rejoicing? Their cause has won.

Check In What strategies did women use to win the vote?

Rosa Parks Says No

by Brinda Gupta

On December 1, 1955, a black woman named Rosa Parks took a seat on a bus in Montgomery, Alabama. As the bus filled with people, a white man told her to get up. He wanted her seat. "No, I will not," Parks replied.

In 1955, different races weren't treated equally in the United States. In the South, **segregation**, or separation among the races, was the law. Black passengers had to sit in the back of the bus. If the front seats filled up, white passengers could force black passengers to give up their seats to them. Black passengers who refused were breaking segregation laws.

Rosa Parks had long fought for African American civil rights. But she had never broken the law. "When I made that decision," Parks said later, "I knew that I had the strength of my ancestors with me." Her act was a type of **civil disobedience**, a nonviolent protest against a law or policy.

Her refusal changed history. Her actions helped spark the Civil Rights Movement, a struggle to win equal rights for African Americans. The Civil Rights Movement brought African Americans the rights of full citizenship guaranteed in the Fourteenth Amendment. It also helped African Americans win the vote, as promised by the Fifteenth Amendment.

Rosa Parks poses for a photo on a bus much like the one she had boarded when she refused to give up her seat.

"I knew someone had to take the first step, and I made up my mind not to move. Our mistreatment was just not right, and I was tired of it." —ROSA PARKS

> During the bus boycott, people often walked to work in the rain.

Boycott!

When African Americans in Montgomery heard Parks's story, they knew they had to support her. They were fed up with segregation. Civil rights groups decided to stage a **boycott** of the Montgomery buses until the laws were changed. During a boycott, people refuse to buy a good or service in order to make a point. In Montgomery, African Americans made up 75 percent of the total passengers on the buses. The bus fares they paid helped run the city. What better way of sending a

Few people rode the buses in Montgomery during the boycott. As a result, the bus companies lost more and more money.

message to the bus companies and the city than to stop using the buses?

The boycott took a lot of planning. People with cars gave rides to former bus riders. Many people walked instead of riding the bus. Even in bad weather and over long distances, people walked to work, school, and elsewhere. The first day of the boycott was a success. Lines of walkers snaked through the city past empty buses. Leaders asked people to keep it up, and the Montgomery bus boycott lasted 381 days.

"She Helped Change America"

The boycott hurt Montgomery and the bus companies, but the city and state did not want to let go of the segregation laws. Lawyers took the case to the U.S. Supreme Court. They argued that segregation laws went against the Constitution. The Court agreed. On November 13, 1956, it ruled that Montgomery's buses could no longer be segregated. African Americans returned to riding the buses—and they could sit where they pleased.

The Montgomery bus boycott was one of the most successful protests against racial segregation. There was no violence. No property was damaged. People simply chose not to support an unjust system.

Parks spent the rest of her life working for civil rights. She has been called the "Mother of the Civil Rights Movement." Parks inspired others by setting a good example. People saw that Parks had made a big difference just by standing up for her beliefs.

This nine-foot-tall statue in Washington, D.C., honors Rosa Parks.